Karen Lynn Slusher is a faith-driven leader and writer with a deep calling to serve people through meaningful, purpose-filled work. Whether leading strategic initiatives or supporting her local church, she brings warmth, wisdom, and intention to every interaction. Her professional journey is marked by a commitment to cultivating trust, championing ethical leadership, and making healthy, purpose-filled living more accessible to others. Karen lives in the Pacific Northwest with her husband, a retired Army aviator, whose legacy of discipline and love continues to inspire her life and work. *The Radical Thread* is her invitation to reimagine leadership and service as sacred, guided by truth in love.

For my Grandpa, **Ernest Thompson,**
A strong man of faith, a shepherd of souls, and a true pillar of both church and home.

You lived what you preached, with gentleness, love, high expectations, and unwavering devotion to the One you served. You showed me that strength is not loudness, but steadfastness. You taught me that discipline is not cruelty, but care. You modeled a life where ministry was not confined to a pulpit but woven into every moment, every word, every choice.

Your dry humor, your quiet wisdom, your serious heart for the things of God – they shaped me more than you could have known.

When my emotions would overtake my judgment, you would gently remind me, *"Karen Lynn, your reactions are showing."* Words that still guide me to this day.

You helped mold me into the woman I am. Your love and guidance remain stitched into the very fabric of my life. I carry your words in my heart, your faith in my spirit, and your legacy in my leadership.

Though you are with the Lord, you are also here, woven into every thread of this journey. This book, this work, this heart of service, it all carries your fingerprints.

Thank you, Grandpa. I miss you. I honor you. I love you always.

"I have fought the good fight, I have finished the race, I have kept the faith." *2 Timothy 4:7 (NIV)*

Karen Lynn Slusher

THE RADICAL THREAD

Weaving Faith, Love, and Service into the Customer Experience

AUSTIN MACAULEY PUBLISHERS®

LONDON * CAMBRIDGE * NEW YORK * SHARJAH

Ordering Information
Quantity sales: Special discounts are available on quantity purchases by corporations, associations, and others. For details, contact the publisher at the address below.

Publisher's Cataloging-in-Publication data
Slusher, Karen Lynn
The Radical Thread

ISBN 9781685629014 (Paperback)
ISBN 9781685629021 (Hardback)
ISBN 9798886932669 (ePub e-book)

Library of Congress Control Number: 2026904173

www.austinmacauleyusa.com

First Published 2026
Austin Macauley Publishers LLC
40 Wall Street, 33rd Floor, Suite 3302
New York, NY 10005
USA

mail-usa@austinmacauley.com
+1 (646) 5125767

This book would not exist without the encouragement, support, and wisdom of several people who walked alongside me during its creation.

I am deeply grateful to Pete Strayer, fellow writer, peer, trusted friend, and brother in Christ, whose steady encouragement gave me the courage to begin and the resolve to finish.

My sincere thanks to the colleagues who took the time to read early drafts, ask thoughtful questions, and offer honest, valuable feedback. Your insights strengthened both the words on these pages and the heart behind them.

Most of all, I thank my husband, Mike, for his unwavering support and love throughout this journey. Your presence, encouragement, and belief in me made this work possible in more ways than you know.

Table of Contents

Introduction
The Radical Thread

There's a thread running through everything we do, whether we see it or not.

It runs through every decision we make, every conversation we engage in, every policy we create, every email we send.

It weaves through the way we greet customers, the way we train teams, the way we lead under pressure.

It even runs through the way we handle mistakes, the way we celebrate success, and the way we correct and restore.

The only question is: what is the thread made of?

For much of my life, I have approached customer experience, leadership, and service like many others do:

- Prioritizing efficiency.
- Chasing excellence.
- Managing problems.
- Celebrating wins.

None of these are wrong.

But they are incomplete without something deeper, something eternal, woven through them.

Because when faith is absent, even the best systems eventually fray. When love is absent, even the smoothest service feels hollow.

When grace is absent, even the most successful leadership leaves people wounded.

It took time, prayer, and failure for me to realize:

Customer experience isn't just about policies and satisfaction surveys. It's about people. It's about ministry. It's about weaving the Kingdom into places the world has left untouched.

This book is born from that realization, and from a deep longing to see faith, love, and service integrated into the fabric of everyday work.

Not tacked on.

Not hidden away for "appropriate" moments.

Not confined to Sunday mornings or personal life.

But woven boldly, faithfully, joyfully into the daily reality of business, service, and leadership.

You hold in your hands a blueprint, but not the kind you might expect.

This isn't a book about better customer service techniques (though there will be plenty of practical tools). This is a book about radical transformation:

- Starting with your heart.
- Flowing into your work.
- Changing the systems around you.
- Building a culture that reflects the heart of God.

Each chapter will walk you through a spiritual principle that reshapes how we serve, lead, and build.

Each chapter will offer practical applications, scripture-centered reflection, and a prayer to root you deeper in Christ.

You don't need to be the CEO to lead this movement.

You don't need to have a title to transform your environment. You just need to be willing to weave the radical thread.

The truth woven through it all is:

When you serve with faith, love, and Spirit-led excellence, your work becomes worship. Your service becomes sacred ground.

And the thread you weave will stretch far beyond what your eyes can see.

Let's pick up the needle. Let's choose the thread.

And let's weave a story worth telling…one stitch of faithfulness, one act of service, one heart at a time.

Welcome to The Radical Thread.

Let's build something beautiful together.

Before You Begin: An Invitation to the 25-Week Radical Thread Challenge

This is not just a book. It's an invitation.

The Radical Thread was written to weave deep faith, radical love, and Spirit-led service into every layer of your work, leadership, and life. But transformation doesn't happen overnight, it happens over time, through   reflection, prayer, obedience, and action.

That's why this book is designed as a 25-Week Challenge.

Each chapter represents a weekly focused opportunity to pause, examine, pray, and intentionally apply a Kingdom principle to your work and leadership.

You are invited to journey slowly and faithfully:

- One chapter per week.
- One heart posture to reflect and pray over.
- One practical act of radical service to live out.
- One Scripture to anchor your leadership for the week.

Why 25 weeks?

Because true discipleship isn't rushed.

- 25 weeks (approximately six months) gives time for deep roots to grow.
- It allows you to actually *implement* each principle into the rhythms of your leadership, service, and daily work life.
- And it matches the way real faith-based growth happens: slow, intentional, heart-deep, just like the Kingdom of God grows in the soil of surrender and steadfastness.

Whether you walk through this journey alone, with your team, or with a community of believers, allow these 25 weeks to become a sacred season:

- To reframe your work as worship.
- To restore the weary places in your leadership and service.
- To root yourself deeper in the true Source of lasting impact, Jesus Christ.
- To realign your heart to Heaven's rhythms.

This is a season of weaving.

One faithful thread at a time.

At the end of these 25 weeks, may your leadership reflect gentleness wrapped in strength, your service carry the fragrance of Christ, and your legacy bear the unmistakable mark of Heaven touching Earth.

Let's begin.

Part 1
The Foundation – Faith-Driven CX Mindset

Chapter 1
The Call to Abundance

Spiritual Principle: *God's provision is abundant; we serve from fullness, not fear.*

Scripture Anchor: 'The thief comes only to steal and kill and destroy; I came that they may have life, and have it abundantly.' – John 10:10 (ESV)

Most customer experience books begin with a focus on satisfaction. Metrics. Loyalty. Efficiency. But as believers, our approach must begin somewhere different, *with the heart of God.*

When Jesus spoke of "abundant life," He wasn't talking about wealth or luxury. He was speaking of a life rooted in Him, full, free, and flourishing. A life where peace surpasses understanding. Where joy isn't tied to circumstance. Where service becomes a sacred act. This kind of abundance isn't accidental. It's intentional. It's radical. And it changes everything, even how we serve people in business.

In today's marketplace, scarcity thinking is everywhere. Companies cut corners. People expect disappointment. Customers arrive guarded. But Kingdom people are called to a different standard. We are called to embody abundance, not just offer it.

Abundance looks like:

- Listening with patience, even when it's inconvenient.
- Giving generously, even when it isn't "required."
- Lifting burdens, even when they're not ours to carry.

Abundance says, 'I see you. You matter. You're worth more than the transaction.'

There was a time I answered a customer message late at night. It wasn't urgent by business standards, but something in my spirit said this mattered. The person on the other end had lost a child and was grasping for something steady. She didn't need a policy. She needed presence. I sat in silence. I cried for her. I prayed over her name. That night wasn't about customer service, it was about communion. That's what abundance does. It turns the ordinary into sacred space.

This chapter is a call, not just to inspire abundant living in others, but to first *receive it for yourself.* Because we can't give what we haven't tasted. And abundant customer experience must flow from an abundant inner life. A life marked by connection to the Vine.

So, I ask you: What are you rooted in? Scarcity or sufficiency? Stress or surrender? Performance or Presence?

Jesus came to give life, not in portions, but in overflow. And if we are to be His ambassadors in business, then we must become living testimonies of that abundance. Even in how we return a call. Even in how we write an email. Even in how we answer frustration with gentleness.

The world doesn't need more fast service. It needs more faithful servants. Abundance is not an outcome. It's a way of being.

And in customer experience, it's the only way that truly satisfies.

Study Guide: Living the Call to Abundance

Key Scriptures to Meditate On:

- John 10:10 – *What does "abundant life" mean to me today?*
- Psalm 23:1 – *"The Lord is my shepherd; I shall not want."*
- 2 Corinthians 9:8 – *"God is able to bless you abundantly…"*

Reflection Questions:

1. Where in my life or leadership am I operating from a mindset of scarcity?
2. When was the last time I offered someone my *presence*, not just a solution?
3. How can I shift the way I serve or lead others to reflect God's abundance?
4. Have I experienced the abundant life Jesus promises, or am I just surviving?
5. Who is one person this week I can serve in a way that reminds them they are seen and valued?

Practical Application:

- Identify one routine task in your work (e.g., responding to a customer email, leading a meeting, helping a colleague) and ask: *How can I do this with the spirit of abundance?* Then do it with intentionality.
- Keep a journal for one week titled *The Overflow List*, every time you experience God's abundance (a moment of peace, provision, wisdom, or joy), write it down. Watch how it shifts your perspective.

———————— ✦ ————————

Prayer

Lord, thank You for the promise of abundant life. Help me not only to receive it but to reflect it. May I be a vessel of Your love in every interaction. Root me in Your presence, so my work is filled with overflow, not striving. Use my hands, my words, my decisions to point people back to You. Amen.

———————— ✦ ————————

Chapter 2
The Weight of Service

Spiritual Principle: *True service carries holy weight, and God strengthens those He calls.*

Scripture Anchor: '**Whatever you do, work heartily, as for the Lord and not for men.' – Colossians 3:23 (ESV)**

Some people see customer service as the entry-level department. The front line. The complaint inbox. A script to follow and a box to check.

But in the Kingdom of God, service is never small. It is weighty. It is sacred. And it is often the very place where heaven touches earth.

We may think of service as a job function, but Scripture paints a different picture: service is *worship*. When done with the right heart, even the most routine act, answering a phone call, packing a box, solving a problem, becomes an offering. A living sacrifice.

The world often ranks people by role. But Jesus flipped that structure completely. In John 13, the Son of God knelt to wash the feet of His disciples. *Dirty feet. Dusty roads. An act reserved for the lowest in the house.* And yet, He called it the way of leadership. The way of love.

In a service role, it's easy to feel invisible. Underappreciated. Overwhelmed. But let me remind you: Jesus sees every act of kindness. Every time you choose grace over frustration. Every time you hold your tongue. Every time you pray over a customer without them knowing. These are not wasted moments. They are holy ones.

True service is not a means to an end. It *is* the ministry.

But let's be honest, it's hard. People are impatient. Systems are broken. You will face accusations that aren't fair. And in those moments, you'll be tempted to respond from the flesh.

That's when we remember *who* we serve.

When you work "as unto the Lord," it doesn't mean you ignore injustice or let people mistreat you. It means your posture is set. You don't serve for applause. You serve from a place of identity, knowing that your reward is eternal, and your value is secure.

Let your standard be higher than the world's because your audience is greater than the customer. It's the King.

Study Guide: The Weight of Service Key Scriptures to Meditate On:

- Colossians 3:23 – *Work heartily as unto the Lord.*
- John 13:12–17 – *Jesus washes His disciples' feet.*
- Philippians 2:5–7 – *Christ took on the nature of a servant.*

Reflection Questions:

- Do I see my work as worship, or simply as a task to complete?
- When was the last time I found joy in an "invisible" act of service?
- How do I respond when someone treats me unfairly in my role?
- Is my heart posture shaped more by people's opinions or God's presence?
- What might it look like to *wash feet* in my current work environment?

Practical Application:

- Take one task this week that feels mundane, something you usually do automatically, and approach it as   an act of worship. Before you begin, pray over it. Dedicate it to God.
- If you're in a leadership role, find a way to *serve your team this week*, something unexpected, small, and genuine. Be the one who kneels.

———————— ✦ ————————

Prayer

Jesus, You showed us what greatness looks like, not in power, but in humility. Teach me to serve like You. Help me to see the hidden moments as holy ones. Give me strength to carry the weight of service with joy, integrity,   and grace. May my work honor You, even when no one else sees. Amen.

———————— ✦ ————————

Chapter 3
The Ministry of Presence

Spiritual Principle: *Being present is often more powerful than any task performed.*
Scripture Anchor: *'Rejoice with those who rejoice, weep with those who weep.' – Romans 12:15 (ESV)*

Presence is one of the most undervalued assets in today's world.

In a fast-paced, hyper-connected society, it's easy to confuse availability with presence. But being present is not just about showing up, it's about *being fully there*. It's about entering into someone's moment, whether it's joy or grief, and carrying it with them for just a little while.

At its highest calling, customer experience isn't about completing a transaction, it's about embodying love. It's a sacred opportunity to practice *incarnational service*, the kind Jesus modeled when He stepped into our world, took on flesh, and walked among us. He didn't just solve problems from a distance; He entered into them, bringing compassion, presence, and restoration.

Definition:

Incarnational service is the act of serving others by being fully present, empathetic, and engaged, bringing love, truth, and grace into real-world situations with humility and compassion, just as Jesus did when He   entered into humanity.

Key Characteristics

- **Presence over performance** – You show up *with* people, not just *for* them.
- **Empathy before action** – You enter their experience, not just try to fix it.
- **Sacrifice and proximity** – You are willing to be close to mess, pain, or need.
- **Reflecting Christ** – Your actions, tone, and attitude become a living picture of Jesus' heart.

This is what sets Kingdom-centered service apart: we don't run from people's pain or inconvenience, we move toward it. We sit in it. We listen long. And we respond, not from a script, but from compassion.

When a customer is angry, it's often not the issue itself but the feeling of being unseen that fuels their frustration. When a coworker is overwhelmed, they don't need another directive, they need someone who will   understand. In these moments, when we choose to pause, to listen, and to feel with them, we step into their   story. And in doing so, we reflect the very heart of Christ.

Being present doesn't always mean you solve the issue. Sometimes presence is the solution.

In Luke 8, Jesus is walking through a crowd when He's touched by a woman who had been bleeding for twelve years. She doesn't cry out. She doesn't introduce herself. But Jesus stops. *He makes the moment personal.* He doesn't rush past her pain. He notices her. Speaks to her. Restores her.

That is presence.

The world trains us to multitask, to move quickly, to prioritize productivity. But love doesn't rush. Love lingers.

As followers of Christ, we are called to make room. For discomfort. For slow conversations. For inconvenient moments. Because in that sacred pause, people are reminded of their worth, not just to us, but to God.

Study Guide: The Ministry of Presence Key Scriptures to Meditate On:

- Romans 12:15 – *"Rejoice with those who rejoice, weep with those who weep."*
- Luke 8:43–48 – *Jesus stops for the bleeding woman.*
- Job 2:13 – *"They sat with him on the ground seven days and seven nights, and no one spoke a word to him."*

Reflection Questions:

- How often am I truly present in my interactions, with customers, coworkers, even my family?
- What distractions or internal "hurry" keep me from listening deeply?
- When was the last time I simply sat with someone in their frustration, grief, or joy without trying to fix it?
- Have I become more focused on solving problems than seeing people?
- How does Jesus' way of noticing people inspire me to slow down and see more deeply?

Practical Application:

- Practice "Holy Noticing" this week. Choose one person each day to give your full attention to, no phone, no multitasking. Just eye contact, empathy, and presence.
- When a customer or colleague comes to you with an issue, take 10 extra seconds to pause and silently pray, "Lord, help me see them as You do." Then respond.

————— ✦ —————

Prayer

Father, help me to be still in a world that rushes. Teach me the power of presence, the kind that doesn't just hear but listens, doesn't just respond but understands. Jesus, you stopped for the one. Help me do the same. Make me attentive to the sacred in every interaction. Let my presence reflect Yours. Amen.

————— ✦ —————

Chapter 4
The Power of Gentle Words

Spiritual Principle: *Gentleness reflects the heart of God and turns away strife.*

Scripture Anchor: 'A gentle answer turns away wrath, but a harsh word stirs up anger.' – Proverbs 15:1 (NIV)

There is a quiet force in this world that can break tension, disarm conflict, and soften even the hardest heart. It's not authority. It's not speed. It's not being "right."

It's gentleness.

In an age that celebrates clever comebacks and reactive outrage, gentleness feels countercultural, maybe even weak. But in the Kingdom of God, gentleness is a fruit of the Spirit and a mark of spiritual maturity. It doesn't avoid hard truth, it delivers it in a way that restores, not wounds.

Customer experience puts you in the crosshairs of other people's stress. Sometimes you will be blamed for things you didn't do. Sometimes you'll be misunderstood. Sometimes people will be hurting, and they'll use your team as a place to unleash that pain.

And in those moments, your tone becomes your testimony.

I've found that when I lead with a soft tone, even in tense situations, it creates room for peace. It's not about being passive, it's about being Spirit-led. Gentleness doesn't mean you compromise on truth. It means you value the person more than the point.

Jesus modeled this beautifully. In John 8, when a woman caught in adultery is thrown before Him, the crowd demands judgment. Jesus kneels. He doesn't raise His voice. He simply writes in the dirt. Then He speaks with disarming grace: *"Let him who is without sin cast the first stone."* When they all walk away, He turns to the woman and says, *"Neither do I condemn you. Go and sin no more."*

Truth. Grace. Gentleness.

In customer experience, every email, every phone call, every message is a chance to demonstrate what the Holy Spirit sounds like. Will you echo the rage of the world, or will you respond with the voice of Heaven?

Gentleness isn't weakness. It's strength under control. And in the tension of daily service, it is one of our greatest Kingdom tools.

Study Guide: The Power of Gentle Words Key Scriptures to Meditate On:

- Proverbs 15:1 – *A gentle answer turns away wrath.*
- Galatians 5:22–23 – *The fruit of the Spirit includes gentleness.*
- Philippians 4:5 – *"Let your gentleness be evident to all. The Lord is near."*

Reflection Questions:

1. When I feel attacked or stressed, what is my natural tone? Defensive? Calm? Dismissive?

2. How would people describe the "voice" of my communication, both spoken and written?
3. Can I recall a time when a gentle word shifted an entire conversation? What made it powerful?
4. What habits can I build to respond in the Spirit, rather than reacting in the flesh?
5. Have I mistaken gentleness for weakness in myself or others?

Practical Application:

- For the next week, before responding to any challenging customer or coworker message, pause and pray: *"Holy Spirit, guide my tone."* Then write or speak with gentleness.
- Begin tracking situations where your calm response shifted the tone of the conversation. Reflect at the end of the week on how gentleness became your witness.

———————— ✦ ————————

Prayer

Lord, teach me to be gentle the way You are gentle, with strength, with grace, and with patience. Help me resist the urge to react and instead respond with Your Spirit. May my words heal, not harm. May my tone reflect the nearness of Your presence. Let my gentleness be my testimony. Amen.

———————— ✦ ————————

Chapter 5
Grace in the Tension

Spiritual Principle: *Grace transforms conflict into connection*

Scripture Anchor: '**But he said to me, 'My grace is sufficient for you, for my power is made perfect in weakness.' – 2 Corinthians 12:9 (ESV)**

Conflict is inevitable. In life. In leadership. In service. There will be moments when your values are questioned, your decisions misunderstood, and your heart misread. And in customer experience, you may face more conflict in a single day than some people experience in a month.

But the Kingdom response to conflict is not to retaliate, it is to redeem.

Grace is the spiritual principle that changes everything in the midst of tension. Grace says: *You may not deserve kindness right now, but I'll offer it anyway. You may be wrong, but I will speak to you with honor. You may be frustrated, but I will not meet your fire with fire.*

Grace is not tolerance. It doesn't ignore injustice or error. But it *enters the tension with truth and mercy held together.*

I remember a moment when a customer sent a furious email, filled with accusation, profanity, and assumptions. My first instinct was to correct them. To defend. But the Spirit quieted me, and I simply replied with compassion. I acknowledged their frustration, gently clarified the facts, and then thanked them for giving us the opportunity to make it right. The reply I got was three words: *'I'm so sorry.'*

That's what grace does. It softens what's hardened, unsettles confusion with clarity, and brings calm where emotions once ran high.

Jesus did this repeatedly. When Peter cut off the servant's ear in the Garden of Gethsemane, Jesus didn't chastise the servant. Nor did He celebrate Peter's "loyalty." He healed. He restored. Right in the middle of betrayal and injustice, He extended grace.

In the world of Customer Experience, we must become fluent in grace. Not just because it feels good, but because it *frees people*. And that includes us.

Without grace, we grow bitter. Defensive. Hardened by daily friction. But with grace, we stay soft. Teachable. Useful to the Master.

You may not always win the argument. But if you walk away having extended grace, you've already won something far more eternal.

Study Guide: Grace in the Tension Key Scriptures to Meditate On:

- 2 Corinthians 12:9 – *"My grace is sufficient for you."*
- Proverbs 19:11 – *"It is to one's glory to overlook an offense."*
- Luke 23:34 – *"Father, forgive them, for they know not what they do."*

Reflection Questions:

- How do I typically respond when someone challenges, criticizes, or offends me?
- Do I equate grace with weakness, or do I see it as strength under the authority of Christ?
- What situations in my recent work have been opportunities for grace, but I responded with defensiveness instead?
- How does receiving God's grace daily empower me to extend it to others, even difficult ones?
- What might change in my customer relationships if grace became my default?

Practical Application:

- This week, identify one moment of friction (customer or internal) and *choose* grace, respond slowly,   speak kindly, and prioritize restoration over resolution.
- Write out a prayer of grace over someone who has wronged you in the past. You don't need to send it,   just surrender the offense to God.

---- ✦ ----

Prayer

Father, Your grace meets me every day where I fall short. Help me to extend that same grace to others, especially when I'm wronged, misunderstood, or challenged. Teach me to respond with compassion, not pride.   May the way I handle conflict be a testimony of Your mercy and redemption. Let grace rule my words, my tone,   and my posture. Amen.

---- ✦ ----

Chapter 6
Truth in Love

Spiritual Principle: Honesty and compassion are not opposites, they are partners in transformation Scripture Anchor: 'Instead, speaking the truth in love, we will grow to become in every respect the mature body of him who is the head, that is, Christ.' – Ephesians 4:15 (NIV)

Truth without love wounds. Love without truth withers.

But truth in love? That changes people.

Customer Experience demands communication, often difficult, often misunderstood, and often emotionally charged. Whether you're correcting an error, enforcing a policy, or navigating feedback, you stand in a sacred space: the space between truth and love.

The world teaches us to choose. Be the bold truth-teller or the soft-hearted peacemaker. But Jesus doesn't ask us to choose. He asks us to combine.

Ephesians 4:15 tells us to speak the truth in love so that we may grow. That growth isn't just for the person we're talking to, it's for us, too. Telling the truth requires courage. Doing it in love requires character.

Sometimes the most loving thing we can do is to tell a customer: 'This product isn't the right fit for your needs.'

'I understand your concern, but the refund cannot be issued under this policy.' 'I hear your frustration, and I care about your experience, but here's the reality.'

And it's not just with customers. Team members need truth in love too. Correction without shame. Accountability with dignity. Feedback offered not to control, but to call forth the best in someone.

Jesus modeled this masterfully. When He encountered the woman at the well (John 4), He told her the truth about her life… five husbands and the man she was with now wasn't her husband. But He didn't shame her. He didn't lecture. He *invited* her to living water. He saw her. He valued her. And He told her the truth *in love*. The result? Transformation.

Truth in love is more than a communication tactic, it is a ***discipleship discipline***. It requires prayer, humility, timing, and Spirit-led wisdom. It's not about winning arguments or managing appearances; it's about being formed into the kind of person who reflects Jesus in both courage and compassion. This discipline teaches us to value relationship over control and long-term impact over immediate reaction. It reshapes how we lead, how we speak, and how we love.

The goal is not just to be right, it's to be righteous. Not just to correct, but to connect.

Not just to speak, but to build up.

And when we do that, customer experience becomes more than communication. It becomes communion.

What is a Discipleship Discipline?

A **discipleship discipline** is a spiritual practice that forms us into the likeness of Christ – not just in what we believe, but in how we live, lead, speak, and serve.

It is an intentional habit rooted in Scripture and powered by the Spirit, designed to train our hearts toward obedience, humility, and Kingdom impact.

Discipleship disciplines often require:

- **Prayer** – for wisdom, timing, and alignment with God's will
- **Humility** – to let go of pride or the need to be right
- **Practice** – because growth happens through repeated faithfulness
- **Surrender** – trusting God for the fruit, not forcing the outcome

Study Guide: Truth in Love Key Scriptures to Meditate On:

- Ephesians 4:15 – *"Speak the truth in love…"*
- Proverbs 27:6 – *"Wounds from a friend can be trusted."*
- John 4:1–26 – *Jesus and the woman at the well*

Reflection Questions

1. Do I tend to lean more toward truth or love when I communicate difficult things?
2. Have I avoided speaking truth in order to keep the peace, only to realize it created more harm later?
3. How can I ensure my truth-telling builds, rather than breaks?
4. What role does prayer play in preparing me to have hard conversations?
5. When have I experienced someone speaking truth in love to me? What made it powerful?

Practical Application

- This week, write down a situation that requires a hard conversation, with a customer, team member, or peer. Before you speak, pray. Then script out your response with both clarity and kindness.
- Invite accountability: ask a trusted friend or mentor to listen to how you're expressing truth in a challenging situation and provide feedback on whether your tone reflects love.

———————◆———————

Prayer

Father, give me the courage to speak the truth and the compassion to speak it in love. Help me resist the urge to control through words, and instead build bridges that lead to growth. Let my communication reflect the character of Christ, bold, gentle, and full of grace. Teach me to speak with conviction and care, so that every word brings light, healing, and truth. Amen.

———————◆———————

Chapter 7
The Beauty of Endurance

Spiritual Principle: *Faithful service is not flashy, it's steadfast*
   Scripture Anchor: 'Let us not grow weary of doing good, for in due season we will reap, if we do not give up.'
– Galatians 6:9 (ESV)

Some days, customer experience feels like running a marathon without a finish line. The emails don't stop. The same questions repeat. The fires keep flaring up. And no one claps for the one who quietly holds the line day after day.

But the Kingdom sees endurance differently.

Scripture never glorifies speed. It celebrates faithfulness. The long walk. The daily discipline. The one who   stays when it's hard, loves when it's inconvenient, and chooses excellence when no one is watching.

Endurance is more than grit. It's grace with a backbone.

Jesus showed us this when He washed the disciples' feet, all of them, even Judas. He healed on the Sabbath, knowing it would trigger confrontation. He stayed present with people who misunderstood Him, demanded   from Him, betrayed Him. And He went all the way to the cross, enduring the suffering. not because it was easy,   but because love finishes what it starts.

In customer service, endurance looks like:

- Showing up on the hard days with your heart still open.
- Listening with patience for the fiftieth time in one day.
- Refusing to let cynicism harden your spirit.
- Committing to excellence when no one sees.

It also looks like investing in growth, even when it's slow. That's why I believe in equipping teams not just with tools, but with training that fuels endurance, like our ESL and Spanish classes, designed to help employees   connect across language barriers. It's slow work. But it's the kind of work that builds bridges and breaks barriers long-term.

When we endure, we plant seeds that we may never see grow, but God does.

We often think burnout means we're doing too much. Sometimes, it means we're doing the right things from the wrong source. Endurance without intimacy with Christ will always deplete you. But when your strength comes   from the Spirit, your capacity expands beyond your natural limit.

The world values urgency. God values *unyielding faithfulness*.

So don't quit. Don't rush. Don't water down your purpose just because it's hard. Keep sowing. Keep showing up. Because in due season, you will reap.

Study Guide: The Beauty of Endurance Key Scriptures to Meditate On:

- Galatians 6:9 – *"Do not grow weary of doing good…"*

- Hebrews 12:1–2 – *"…run with endurance the race set before us."*
- James 1:12 – *"Blessed is the one who perseveres under trial…"*

Reflection Questions

- Where do I feel most weary in my service or leadership role right now?
- Am I enduring out of obligation, or am I drawing strength from intimacy with Christ?
- What does it look like to serve with consistency, not just intensity?
- How can I lead or encourage others toward long-term faithfulness, not quick wins?
- Are there any rhythms in my life that need to change so that I can endure well?

Practical Application

- **Establish a "rhythm of renewal."** Even God rested on the seventh day, not because He was tired, but to demonstrate the sacred value of rest. He wove renewal into the rhythm of creation itself. Whether it's a walk at lunch, silent prayer before your shift, or a 24-hour tech Sabbath each week, build rest into your routine so you can serve from overflow, not exhaustion.
- **Encourage quiet endurance.** Write a note or message to a teammate or staff member who has quietly served with consistency. Acknowledge their endurance. Encourage their spirit. Let them know their faithfulness hasn't gone unseen.

———————— ✦ ————————

Prayer

Lord, You are the God who never grows weary. Help me to reflect that same faithfulness in my service. Teach me to endure, not out of striving, but out of trust. Fill my spirit with fresh strength each day. Let me be the kind of servant who finishes well. Help me stay rooted in You, so that no storm can shake me. Amen.

———————— ✦ ————————

Chapter 8
The Strength of Joy

Spiritual Principle: *Joy is not optional, it's essential*

Scripture Anchor: *'The joy of the Lord is your strength.' – Nehemiah 8:10 (ESV)*

Joy is not a bonus emotion for the days when everything goes well. It is the fuel for the days when nothing goes as planned.

In customer experience, there are days when nothing goes right. Orders are delayed. Systems break. Tempers flare. If our strength comes from the satisfaction of others or the smoothness of the day, we will collapse. But if our strength comes from the joy of the Lord, then we become people who can serve with consistency, even in chaos.

Joy is not the same as happiness. Happiness is reactive. Joy is resilient. Happiness depends on outcomes. Joy depends on intimacy with God.

The prophet Nehemiah spoke those powerful words, "The joy of the Lord is your strength", to a group of people who were weeping as they heard the law read aloud. They were convicted. Overwhelmed. And instead of telling them to stay in sorrow, Nehemiah told them to celebrate. To feast. To remember that even in the heaviness of their journey, God's joy would sustain them.

That same principle applies to us.

You don't have to wait for ideal circumstances to serve with joy. In fact, joy often shines brightest when it's chosen in the midst of challenge, not comfort. Joy, when expressed in service, is contagious. It lifts customers out of anxiety. It encourages weary teammates. It shifts the tone of an entire day.

Joy says: *Even if this is hard, I choose to carry it with lightness. I choose to reflect something deeper than the moment.*

There was a time I watched a team member deal with a flood of complaints. It was a rough day. But she kept smiling, not forced, not fake. Just present. Warm. Joyful. She ended one call by saying, "I hope you have a truly blessed day. You've been heard." And the customer's entire tone shifted. That's the power of joy. It doesn't just hold us up, it lifts others too.

In a world where cynicism is normal and burnout is glorified, joy is radical. And in customer experience, radical is exactly what's needed.

Study Guide: The Strength of Joy Key Scriptures to Meditate On:

- Nehemiah 8:10 – *"The joy of the Lord is your strength."*
- John 15:11 – *"I have told you this so that my joy may be in you…"*
- Romans 12:12 – *"Be joyful in hope, patient in affliction, faithful in prayer."*

Reflection Questions

1. What has been my source of strength lately, results, approval, or God's joy?

2. When was the last time I felt joy in the middle of a hard day? What helped?
3. Do I unintentionally equate seriousness with professionalism? How can I allow more joy in my leadership or service style?
4. How can I help cultivate a culture of joy in my team or organization?
5. Is there anything stealing my joy right now that I need to surrender to God?

Practical Application

- Begin each workday this week by thanking God for three things before checking your inbox. Watch how gratitude awakens joy.
- Bring a moment of joy to someone else's day, a short encouraging note, a small gift, a kind word. Serve from overflow.

———————— ✦ ————————

Prayer

God, restore to me the joy of Your salvation. Let Your joy be the strength I stand on, not just when things go well, but when they don't. Teach me to carry joy as a banner of faith, visible, steady, and rooted in You. May joy mark my service, brighten my words, and reflect the freedom I've found in You. Amen.

———————— ✦ ————————

Chapter 9
The Freedom of Forgiveness

Spiritual Principle: *Forgiveness is the pathway to freedom, for you and for them*

Scripture Anchor: 'Be kind and compassionate to one another, forgiving each other, just as in Christ God forgave you.' – Ephesians 4:32 (NIV)

You will be wronged in customer experience.

You will be misunderstood, misquoted, and misjudged.

You will pour your heart into serving others, and someone will still walk away angry.

And sometimes, it won't be a customer at all.

It might be a teammate, a boss, a vendor, or even a friend.

The question is not *if* you'll need to forgive. The question is: *Will you choose to?*

Forgiveness is not optional for those who follow Christ, it is foundational.

We don't stand in God's grace because we earned it. We stand because, while we were still sinners, Christ forgave us from the cross (Romans 5:8, Luke 23:34).

And we are called to do the same.

"Be kind and compassionate to one another, forgiving each other, just as in Christ God forgave you."

Ephesians 4:32

So, when forgiveness feels hard, when you'd rather justify your anger than release it, remember:

If God forgave us for Christ's sake, who are we to withhold forgiveness from others?

Forgiveness is not weakness.

It's strength that trusts God with justice while choosing love. It's the thread that mends what offense tears apart.

And it's one of the most powerful ways we reflect Jesus, in leadership, in service, and in every relationship we touch.

Many people don't associate forgiveness with business. But customer experience is full of opportunities for forgiveness:

- The customer who falsely accuses you.
- The coworker who gossips behind your back.
- The leader who overlooks your work.
- The team member who repeatedly misses the mark. Forgiveness doesn't ignore hurt. It releases its hold.

Unforgiveness is a slow toxin, it clouds your perspective, hardens your tone, and eventually leaks into how you serve. That's why Jesus was so direct: forgive. Seventy times seven. Not just for their sake, but for yours.

I once carried resentment toward someone who'd been deeply unfair and hurtful. Every time I tried to serve with joy, I felt that weight pulling me back. Then one day, God whispered: *'You're giving them power over your Worship.'*

That broke my heart. I realized forgiveness isn't just a relational act, it's a spiritual discipline. It clears the   channel between you and God. It reopens the path for joy, peace, and presence.

Forgiveness also shapes how you design your customer experience. Is your policy one of punishment or redemption? Do your people feel empowered to offer grace when appropriate? Are you willing to restore a relationship after failure?

When we reflect the forgiving nature of Christ in how we lead, speak, serve, and operate, we make room for healing.

The truth is, forgiveness will cost you something. But not forgiving will cost you far more.

Study Guide: The Freedom of Forgiveness Key Scriptures to Meditate On

- Ephesians 4:32 – *"Forgiving one another, just as God in Christ forgave you."*
- Matthew 18:21–22 – *"Lord, how often shall I forgive…?"*
- Luke 6:37 – *"Forgive, and you will be forgiven."*

Reflection Questions

1. Is there anyone I need to forgive right now in my work life, customer, colleague, or leader?
2. Have I allowed unforgiveness to affect my tone, decision-making, or ability to serve joyfully?
3. What would it look like to build forgiveness into our team culture?
4. How has God's forgiveness of me shaped the way I extend grace to others?
5. Am I quick to extend forgiveness when someone fails or do I quietly hold it against them?

Practical Application

- Write a letter of forgiveness to someone who's hurt you in your professional life. You don't need to send it, this is for your freedom. Release the weight.
- As a leader, if appropriate, publicly model forgiveness by extending grace to someone who has owned a mistake. Let others see that love covers a multitude of wrongs.

————— ✦ —————

Prayer

Father, thank You for forgiving me again and again. Help me not to hold on to what You've let go of. Teach me to forgive as an act of worship, not because it's easy, but because it reflects Your heart. Cleanse my spirit from bitterness. Heal what's been broken. Let my service flow from a place of freedom, not offense. In Jesus' name, amen.

————— ✦ —————

Chapter 10
Anchored by the Spirit, Positioned for Impact

Spiritual Principle: *Spiritual transformation always leads to practical expression*

Scripture Anchor: 'But the fruit of the Spirit is love, joy, peace, patience, kindness, goodness, faithfulness, gentleness, self-control…' – Galatians 5:22–23 (ESV)

The first steps of this journey have been deeply personal. We've been asked to reflect, to surrender, to receive. To examine our posture. To align our motives.

To soften what life has hardened.

We've explored abundance, integrity, grace, gentleness, truth, endurance, joy, and forgiveness, not as inspirational ideas, but as spiritual imperatives for anyone called to serve.

But the fruit of the Spirit doesn't exist just to make us *nicer people*. It exists to make us Kingdom Carriers.

People who bring the culture of Heaven into everyday places.

What Is a Kingdom Carrier?

A **Kingdom Carrier** is a Spirit-filled believer who brings the presence, values, and culture of God's Kingdom into the spaces they occupy, workplaces, homes, teams, communities. They don't just *represent* the Kingdom; they *carry* it in their words, actions, and atmosphere.

They embody the fruit of the Spirit not for self-improvement, but for **Kingdom impact**, revealing what Heaven looks like on earth through love, joy, peace, patience, kindness, goodness, faithfulness, gentleness, and self-control (Galatians 5:22–23).

In customer experience, that means the fruit of the Spirit doesn't stop at our character, it spills into our decisions, systems, and culture:

- How do we structure policy in a way that reflects patience and kindness?
- How do we train teams to respond with self-control and gentleness?
- How do we build procedures rooted in faithfulness, not fear?
- How do we model peace when tensions are high?

Fruit is evidence of the root.

And if we've been rooted in the Spirit through the first part of this journey, then what comes next must bear evidence of that, *in the way we lead, operate, build, and respond.*

I've watched culture change in an organization, not because we launched a new software or wrote a new handbook, but because one team member began to live out these spiritual principles. Her grace was contagious. Her joy stirred hearts. Her forgiveness healed tension. That's what happens when the Spirit leads, it *spreads.*

As we prepare to move into the next section of this book, I want to offer this reminder: You don't need to be in charge to lead.

You don't need a title to shift culture.

You just need to be anchored in the Spirit, and obedient in the little.

The fruit of the Spirit doesn't depend on your environment. It thrives in whatever soil you're willing to surrender to God.

So ask yourself: How will I carry this into systems, conversations, and culture? How will my customer experience work reflect the invisible hand of a living God?

You've been transformed on the inside. Now let's start weaving it on the outside.

Study Guide: Anchored by the Spirit, Positioned for Impact Key Scriptures to Meditate On

- Galatians 5:22–23 – *"The fruit of the Spirit is…"*
- Matthew 7:16 – *"By their fruit you will recognize them."*
- James 2:17 – *"Faith by itself, if it does not have works, is dead."*

Reflection Questions

1. Which fruit of the Spirit have I most seen God developing in me during this journey?
2. Which one is still a struggle? What might be hindering its growth?
3. How have these inner transformations already affected how I serve others?
4. In what areas of my team, system, or workplace culture do I sense the Spirit inviting me to make a shift?
5. Am I willing to let my actions and decisions bear visible fruit, even if I'm the only one doing so?

Practical Application

- Choose one fruit of the Spirit to intentionally cultivate this week. Ask the Holy Spirit to give you daily opportunities to practice it, and journal what happens.
- Host a short devotional or "Spirit in Service" reflection with your team, if appropriate. Invite others into the journey of weaving faith into their service.

Prayer

Holy Spirit, You are the source of every good and lasting change. Thank You for shaping my heart through this journey. Now anchor me so deeply in You that my words, my work, and my decisions bear lasting fruit. Let my life be evidence of Your presence. Help me, not just to be transformed, but to bring transformation. Wherever I serve, may Heaven be seen. Amen.

Part 2

The Practice – Building Kingdom Culture Through Service, Where We Move from The Heart to The Hands, From Who We Are Becoming to What We Are Building.

Chapter 11
Leadership as Stewardship

Spiritual Principle: *You don't own people, you steward their purpose*

Scripture Anchor: 'Who then is the faithful and wise servant, whom the master has put in charge of the servants in his household…? Blessed is that servant whom his master will find doing so when he comes.' – Matthew 24:45–46 (CSB)

The world often views leadership as control. Power. Position. But in the Kingdom of God, leadership is stewardship.

It's not about ownership, it's about care and service to others.

You may lead a team of two or a company of two hundred. You may oversee call flows, feedback loops, hiring processes, or lunch breaks. But no matter how big or small your role, the principle remains: these people do not belong to you. They belong to God. And your role is to help uncover and nurture the purpose He's placed inside them.

Stewardship means you treat people as sacred trust. It means you don't lead for ego, you lead for growth.

It means you measure success not only by results, but by how your people are flourishing.

In Matthew 24, Jesus speaks of a "faithful and wise servant" who has been entrusted with the care of others. The reward wasn't in how impressive his title was, but in his faithfulness to do what mattered when no one was watching.

Leadership as stewardship means:

- Asking, *"What does this person need to grow?"* not *"What do I need to get from them?"*
- Designing systems that nurture people's growth while still honoring results.
- Seeing beyond performance and into purpose.

I once watched a leader correct a team member who had made a serious mistake. He had every right to discipline. But instead of lashing out, he pulled the person aside and said, *'This doesn't change how I see your potential. Let's work through it.'* The employee walked away not only accountable but inspired. That's stewardship.

When we lead with a heart to serve and steward others, we shift the culture from fear to freedom. People stop hiding. They stop putting on a performance. They start growing. And the entire organization becomes a garden of purpose.

This is especially critical in customer experience roles, positions that are often emotionally taxing and undervalued. When leaders steward their team with honor, the fruit shows up in every customer interaction.

People who feel seen serve others better.

People who are stewarded well become stewards themselves.

Study Guide: Leadership as Stewardship Key Scriptures to Meditate On:

- Matthew 24:45–46 – *"Who then is the faithful and wise servant…?"*
- 1 Peter 5:2–3 – *"Be shepherds of God's flock… not lording it over those entrusted to you…"*

- Proverbs 27:23 – *"Know well the condition of your flocks…"*

Reflection Questions

1. Do I see the people I lead as assets to manage or as souls to steward?
2. How do I balance accountability with compassion in leadership?
3. What systems or practices in my team culture currently honor people's purpose?
4. Have I made assumptions about someone's value based on performance alone?
5. How can I start creating a safe place for my team to grow, even through failure?

Practical Application

- Identify one person you lead and ask them privately: *"What helps you feel supported and grow in your role?"* Then act on it.
- Review one policy, process, or system in your area of influence and ask: *"Does this reflect stewardship or control?"* Adjust if needed.

———————— ✦ ————————

Prayer

Father, thank You for entrusting me with people, not to own or control, but to love and lead with care. Help me to see those I lead the way You do: as image-bearers full of purpose. Teach me to steward their gifts, honor their journeys, and lead with a heart like Yours. May I be found faithful, even in the hidden places. Amen.

———————— ✦ ————————

Chapter 12
Creating a Culture of Belonging

Spiritual Principle: *Belonging heals what performance can't*
   Scripture Anchor: 'Now you are the body of Christ, and each one of you is a part of it.' – 1 Corinthians 12:27 (NIV)

People don't stay in jobs because of perks, they stay because they feel like they belong.

In a world that increasingly isolates and divides, one of the most radical things you can do as a leader, a teammate, or a company is to create spaces where people feel seen, safe, and significant.

Belonging is more than fitting in. Fitting in says, *'I'll become who you want me to be to stay here.'*

Belonging says, *'You see me as I am, and I still have a seat at the table.'*

This is what the Church is meant to be. And this is what our workplace, especially our customer service teams, can reflect when they are grounded in Kingdom principles.

In 1 Corinthians 12, Paul explains that the body of Christ is made up of many parts, each with its own function, each vital to the whole. The eye can't say to the hand, 'I don't need you.' The foot doesn't become less important because it's not a mouth. That same truth applies to our teams.

In customer experience, certain roles are often dismissed as entry-level or secondary. But the truth is, these are the frontline ministers of your organization. They represent the voice, tone, and heart of your values to the world. If these people do not feel like they belong, the customer won't either.

Belonging is cultivated through:

- Language that affirms identity before evaluating performance.
- Practices that invite voices to be heard, especially from those who often go unnoticed.
- Policies that reflect dignity, not just efficiency.

I've seen belonging flourish in environments where someone said, 'We noticed you,' or, 'You don't have to earn your worth here.' I've also seen teams fall apart under the unspoken message: "Produce or disappear."

Jesus never required people to prove themselves before loving them. He welcomed the broken, the overlooked, the outcast, and then transformed them through relationship.

As a leader or peer, your words carry weight. Your tone sets the atmosphere. And your systems either open the door for belonging, or quietly push people away.

If you want to build a culture that reflects the Kingdom, then start by asking this: Does every person here know they matter, even when they mess up?

Because that's the soil where people don't just survive. They grow.

Study Guide: Creating a Culture of Belonging Key Scriptures to Meditate On:

- 1 Corinthians 12:27 – *"You are the body of Christ…"*
- Romans 12:5 – *"So in Christ we, though many, form one body…"*

- Luke 19:10 – *"For the Son of Man came to seek and save the lost."*

Reflection Questions

1. Does everyone on my team feel like they are truly needed, not just tolerated?
2. What systems or practices might unintentionally communicate "you don't belong"?
3. Have I allowed performance or comparison to become the foundation of acceptance?
4. How can I personally model the belonging Jesus offers in my workplace?
5. When have I most felt a sense of spiritual and emotional belonging? What made it powerful?

Practical Application

- Make space for someone who often feels overlooked. Invite them into a conversation, ask for their insight, or affirm their contribution in front of others.
- At your next team gathering or one-on-one, try this phrase: *'I just want you to know, you're valuable here, and not because of your output.'*

———— ✦ ————

Prayer

Jesus, You welcomed the outsider. You called the forgotten by name. Teach me to do the same. Help me create an atmosphere where people feel Your love through every interaction. May my words and my presence remind others they are wanted, needed, and chosen. Let my team reflect the wholeness of Your body, where every part belongs. Amen.

———— ✦ ————

Chapter 13
The Way Up Is Down

Spiritual Principle: *True authority comes through humility*
Scripture Anchor: *'Whoever wants to become great among you must be your servant.' – Matthew 20:26 (NIV)*

In the Kingdom of God, greatness doesn't look like titles, platforms, or decision-making power. It looks like a towel and a basin.

When Jesus gathered with His disciples before the crucifixion, He didn't give them a masterclass on leadership. He knelt down, poured water, and washed their feet, even the feet of the one who would betray Him. This wasn't symbolic. It was systemic. He was teaching them how His Kingdom works: *the way up is down.*

Too often, leadership in the world is modeled after visibility and control. But in the way of Jesus, leaders serve first. They carry weight that others don't see. They absorb blame when things go wrong. They celebrate others when things go right.

Servant leadership isn't weak. It's wildly courageous. Because it means:

- You lead through influence, not intimidation.
- You put your team's growth above your own comfort.
- You wash feet that are muddy, bruised, or undeserving, and do so without applause.

I've watched teams shift when leadership moved from demanding to *serving.* I've seen hardened attitudes melt under the tenderness of a boss who said, 'How can I serve you today?' I've seen companies grow not because they had flashy strategies, but because their leaders lived low and lifted others high.

The customer experience world is full of hierarchy. Escalations go "up the ladder." Policies are enforced "from the top." But imagine the transformation if every leader, supervisor, manager, or executive saw themselves as the bottom support beam, not the rooftop.

Jesus didn't just preach servant leadership. He lived it. And then He looked His disciples in the eye and said, *'Now that I, your Lord and Teacher, have washed your feet, you also should wash one another's feet'* (John 13:14).

Leadership is not about being impressive. It's about being *available.*

And the most powerful leaders in the Kingdom are often the ones no one notices, because they're too busy serving.

Study Guide: The Way Up Is Down Key Scriptures to Meditate On

- Matthew 20:26–28 – *"Whoever wants to become great…"*
- John 13:1–17 – *Jesus washes the disciples' feet*
- Philippians 2:5–7 – *"He made Himself nothing…"*

Reflection Questions

1. Do I lead from a place of service or status?
2. What does my leadership communicate about what I value, control or care?
3. In what ways can I practically "wash feet" this week for those I lead or serve with?
4. How do I respond when I'm asked to do something beneath my title or role?
5. Have I created space in my team for leadership that looks like Jesus, not just success by worldly standards?

Practical Application

- Choose one act of humble service this week to bless someone you lead, without making it public or expecting thanks.
- Begin one team meeting with this question: *"Is there anything I can do this week to better serve you?"*
- Then listen without defensiveness.

————————— ✦ —————————

Prayer

Jesus, You are the Servant King. You had every right to demand worship, but instead You washed feet. Teach me to lead like You. Strip away my pride, my need to be seen, and my fear of being small. Make me a leader who lifts others. Let my authority be rooted in love, not position. Use my hands for humble service. Use my voice for encouragement. Use my life to reflect Yours. Amen.

————————— ✦ —————————

Chapter 14
Training Hearts, Not Just Hands

Spiritual Principle: *Equipping people in skill and spirit multiplies Kingdom impact*
   Scripture Anchor: 'Whatever you have learned or received or heard from me, or seen in me, put it into practice. And the God of peace will be with you.' – Philippians 4:9 (NIV)

Training is often treated as a checklist. A box to tick before someone's "ready." But in the Kingdom, training is discipleship.

It's not just about what people know, it's about who they're becoming.

In many customer experience settings, team members are handed a script, a software guide, and a performance metric. What's often missing is the why behind the what, and the *heart* behind the how.

The truth is, most service failures aren't due to lack of knowledge. They're the result of burnout, frustration, misunderstanding, or a breakdown in connection. And those issues can't be fixed with technical training alone.

Training that reflects the heart of Christ focuses on:

- Instilling values, not just processes.
- Modeling tone, not just memorizing lines.
- Reinforcing dignity, not just efficiency.
- Tending to the soul, not just the skillset.

In Philippians 4, Paul didn't just say, *'Listen to my words.'* He said, *'Do what you've seen in me.'* That's the kind of training that lasts, the kind that's lived out in front of others, not just taught from a slide deck.

I remember working with a new team member who was technically gifted but unsure of how to de-escalate tough situations. Instead of handing them a flowchart, I invited them to shadow a leader who navigated tension   with grace. Afterward, the new rep said, *'I learned more in 20 minutes listening to their calls than I could've in hours of training.'* Why? Because character is contagious.

Training hearts means building an environment where values are not just words on the wall, they're demonstrated in how leaders respond to failure, how feedback is given, and how expectations are communicated.

It also means creating space for *spiritual growth* within professional development:

- Team devotions or reflection time (when appropriate).
- Encouragement that addresses the person, not just their output.
- Leadership that prays for its people and speaks life into their journey. We are not just raising up workers. We are stewarding image-bearers.

When we train the whole person, heart, mind, and hands, we build teams that don't just survive service… they minister through it.

Study Guide: Training Hearts, Not Just Hands Key Scriptures to Meditate On

- Philippians 4:9 – *"Whatever you have learned… put it into practice."*
- Proverbs 22:6 – *"Train up a child in the way he should go…"*
- 2 Timothy 2:2 – *"…entrust to faithful people who will be able to teach others also."*

Reflection Questions

1. What are the unspoken values people "catch" from me when I train or lead?
2. Do I train for performance or for transformation?
3. How can I model Christ's character more intentionally in my onboarding or coaching processes?
4. What training moments in my past deeply shaped me, and why?
5. Where can I begin integrating heart and spirit into the way I train others?

Practical Application

- Identify one training or onboarding process you oversee and revise it to include not just what to do, but how to do it with love, patience, and humility.
- Invite a seasoned team member who models the company's values to mentor or shadow a newer one, creating a culture of shared discipleship.

———————— ✦ ————————

Prayer

Lord, You are the Master Teacher. You taught not only with words, but with presence, compassion, and example. Help me to train others the way You train me, with grace, truth, and love. Let my instruction point to more than a system; let it reflect Your Spirit. May those I equip be strengthened not just in skill, but in soul. And may everything we do point back to You. Amen.

———————— ✦ ————————

Chapter 15

Designing Systems with a Shepherd's Heart

Spiritual Principle: *Justice, mercy, and truth must live in the structure, not just the slogan*

Scripture Anchor: 'He has shown you, O man, what is good; and what does the Lord require of you? To act justly, to love mercy, and to walk humbly with your God.' – Micah 6:8 (NIV)

Policies are often where the heart of a company is most clearly revealed.

It's easy to craft a brand message that says, *"We care."* But what do your customers and employees encounter when something goes wrong? When they miss a deadline? When they forget the terms? When life interrupts their plans?

Do your systems reflect a God who is just, but also merciful? Do they hold truth without losing tenderness?

Micah 6:8 gives us a blueprint for building anything, including service systems: Act justly. Love mercy. Walk humbly.

In the world, policies are built to protect assets.

In the Kingdom, policies are built to protect people.

This doesn't mean abandoning accountability or stewardship. Quite the opposite. It means designing structure that mirrors the nature of our Shepherd:

- **Justice:** Clear, fair expectations that don't shift with emotion or favoritism.
- **Mercy:** Processes for restoration and exceptions when life breaks the rules.
- **Truth:** Transparency that keeps trust intact, even when the answer is no.

Customer experience is full of tension: What if they're lying? What if we're being taken advantage of? What if offering grace sets a precedent?

Here's the truth: it might. But so does forgiveness. So does foot-washing.

So does Calvary.

Even our internal procedures, metrics, performance reviews, training paths, must echo Kingdom values. Are we measuring what matters? Are we disciplining to restore, or to punish? Are we creating cultures where truth can be spoken in love?

The Shepherd leaves the ninety-nine to find the one.

And He doesn't ask for perfection before bringing them home.

So let's build systems that don't just maintain order but extend invitation.

Study Guide: Designing Systems with a Shepherd's Heart Key Scriptures to Meditate On

- Micah 6:8 – *"Act justly. Love mercy. Walk humbly."*
- Isaiah 30:18 – *"The Lord longs to be gracious to you..."*
- John 10:11 – *"I am the good shepherd..."*

Reflection Questions

1. Do our current service policies reflect God's justice, mercy, and truth?
2. Where are we most tempted to sacrifice mercy for the sake of efficiency?
3. How do our systems treat people when they fail or break a rule?
4. What message do our procedures communicate about who belongs, and who doesn't?
5. Am I willing to revise systems not just for functionality, but for faithfulness?

Practical Application

- Choose one policy or customer-facing process and examine it through the lens of Christ. Ask yourself: *If Jesus were on the receiving end of this, would He feel seen, valued, and treated with compassion and truth?* If not, consider how you might revise the tone, structure, or flexibility to better reflect both grace and truth.
- Host a roundtable with a cross-section of your team and ask: *Where do our systems feel impersonal? How can we build in compassion?*

---------------- ✦ ----------------

Prayer

Shepherd of my soul, You lead with wisdom and compassion. Teach me to build systems that reflect Your heart, firm in truth, soft in mercy, steady in justice. Help me steward policies not as barriers, but as bridges. May every form, rule, and process become a reflection of Your love for Your people. Guide me as I build. Let it all point to You. Amen.

---------------- ✦ ----------------

Chapter 16
Correction That Restores

Spiritual Principle: *Discipline in love creates safety, not shame*

Scripture Anchor: 'Those whom I love I rebuke and discipline. So be earnest and repent.' – Revelation 3:19 (NIV)

In many workplaces, correction is transactional, cold, quick, and often laced with shame. In the Kingdom, correction is relational.

It is given not to tear down, but to build up again the right way.

The Bible is full of correction. Jesus corrected His disciples. The prophets corrected nations. Paul corrected   entire churches. But the thread running through every Spirit-led rebuke is this: love.

"Those whom I love I rebuke and discipline."

Correction should never be driven by embarrassment, annoyance, or a need to control. It should be driven by a desire to see someone restored to truth and excellence, to become who God created them to be.

In customer experience roles, especially those that are high-pressure and fast-paced, there will be mistakes. And as leaders or peers, we have two choices when people fall short:

1. Enforce discipline to maintain fear and order.
2. Offer correction that cultivates trust and accountability.

Correction that reflects Christ:

- Affirms identity before addressing behavior.
- Names the issue clearly but never attacks the person.
- Includes framework for change, not just consequences for error.
- Invites dialogue, growth, and restoration.

I once walked alongside an employee who had developed a pattern of lateness and unresponsiveness. Instead of issuing a formal write-up immediately, I asked to hear their story. We uncovered some deep struggles that were never visible in their performance report. From there, we created a plan, not just for improvement, but for   healing. That person eventually became one of the most consistent and trusted members of the team. Why?

Because correction met compassion.

It's easy to over-correct in the name of excellence or under-correct in the name of grace. But the Kingdom is built on both: truth and love.

You don't have to sacrifice one to uphold the other.

Correction is an act of service. It protects the culture. It guards unity. It calls people higher.   But only when it's rooted in relationship.

Study Guide: Correction That Restores Key Scriptures to Meditate On

- Revelation 3:19 – *"Those whom I love I rebuke and discipline."*
- Proverbs 27:6 – *"Wounds from a friend can be trusted…"*
- Galatians 6:1 – *"Restore them gently…"*

Reflection Questions

1. How do I tend to handle correction? Do I avoid it altogether, deliver it too harshly, or approach it with both truth and love?
2. Do my team members feel safe enough to receive feedback without fear?
3. Have I been corrected in a way that brought growth rather than shame? What made it different?
4. How does Jesus model correction that is both honest and full of grace?
5. Where might God be inviting me to shift my posture or tone when delivering discipline?

Practical Application

- Reflect on a current or past situation where someone under your leadership needed correction. Ask: *Did I approach it with restoration in mind?* If not, make amends where possible.
- Create a "Grace & Growth" framework for team feedback: structure corrections to begin with value, explain behavior, offer a plan, and close with hope.

---------------- ✦ ----------------

Prayer

Lord, You correct me not to condemn me, but to shape me. Teach me to do the same with others. Help me lead with wisdom, grace, and truth. Let my discipline reflect Your heart, not controlling or cold, but full of hope and restoration. May my tone and timing be led by Your Spirit. May those I correct feel loved, not diminished. Help me strive to grow people and glorify Your name. Amen.

---------------- ✦ ----------------

Chapter 17
Measuring What Matters

Spiritual Principle: *Faithfulness is measured in fruit, not just figures*

    Scripture Anchor: *'By their fruit you will recognize them.' – Matthew 7:16 (NIV)*

What gets measured, gets valued. And what gets valued, gets repeated.

That's why the way you measure performance says more about your culture than your mission statement ever could.

In many customer experience organizations, metrics revolve around speed, volume, and productivity:

- Calls answered per hour.
- Average handle time.
- Number of refunds processed.
- Resolution rates.

These metrics have value, they offer insight into flow, function, and efficiency. But in a Kingdom-centered service culture, metrics must go deeper.

They must also reflect:

- Patience.
- Wisdom.
- Kindness.
- Fruitfulness.

Jesus never said, 'You'll know them by their quarterly numbers.' He said, *'You'll know them by their fruit.'*

Fruit isn't just about results, it's about the character and impact that grow over time.

A customer may leave satisfied because their issue was resolved, but were they also treated with gentleness?   With joy? Did they walk away with peace instead of pressure?

The best leaders measure both outcome and atmosphere.

Here's what that could look like in a faith-driven service organization:

- Tracking not just how many issues were resolved, but how many *relationships were restored.*
- Listening not just to words on a survey, but to tone in a voice and spirit in the room.
- Evaluating agents not just by efficiency, but by empathy.
- Asking teams: *What fruit of the Spirit did you notice in your work this week?*
- Inviting reflection: *Can you share a specific moment this week when you helped restore a relationship with a customer, coworker, or partner? What shifted, and how did it feel?*

I remember one leader who created a monthly **"Kingdom KPIs"** reflection, asking each team member to highlight one moment they saw or expressed spiritual fruit in service. It changed everything. Suddenly, the wins weren't just in closing tickets, they were in opening hearts.

When we measure what matters to Heaven, we shape what matters on earth.

We remind our people that their work is not just productivity, it's planting seeds.

Examples of Kingdom KPIs Relational Restoration

- Number of customer relationships repaired after a mistake or miscommunication
- Number of internal conflicts resolved with humility and reconciliation
- Follow-up touchpoints after resolution to ensure the person felt seen and restored

Spiritual Fruit in Action

- Peer-nominated stories of someone living out the fruit of the Spirit (love, joy, peace, patience, etc.)
- Reflections shared in meetings about where team members noticed God at work
- Team check-ins: "Which fruit of the Spirit was most challenging, and most visible, this week?"

Servant Leadership Impact

- Number of moments where someone went above and beyond in unseen service
- Leadership humility markers, such as feedback accepted, apologies offered, or empowerment of others
- Mentorship investment: hours or frequency of pouring into others' growth

Emotional and Spiritual Climate

- "Presence & Peace" score – peer feedback on how peaceful, gracious, and Spirit-led interactions felt
- Tone audits of emails or calls – not just accuracy, but *how* something was said
- Moments of mercy tracked – decisions where grace was chosen over policy

Culture of Generosity

- Number of encouragements or affirmations given to teammates or customers
- Random acts of kindness reported within the workplace
- Time volunteered or causes supported as a team

☐ **Framing Thought:** *Earth measures impact in numbers. Heaven measures impact in fruit.*

Kingdom KPIs help us see the invisible victories, the softened tone, the kind word spoken, the team member uplifted, the angry customer transformed.

Study Guide: Measuring What Matters Key Scriptures to Meditate On

- Matthew 7:16 – *"By their fruit you will recognize them."*
- Colossians 3:23 – *"Work heartily, as for the Lord…"*
- Galatians 5:22–23 – *"The fruit of the Spirit is…"*

Reflection Questions

1. What are the current metrics I use to measure success in my team or work?
2. Do those metrics reflect what truly matters to the Kingdom, or just to our bottom line?
3. What does it look like to measure fruit, like joy, peace, kindness, in a meaningful way?
4. Have I ever performed well on paper while failing to reflect God's character?
5. What conversations could I open with my team about redefining "success"?

Practical Application

- Begin developing a "Kingdom KPI" framework for your team. Include both spiritual and strategic   metrics, fruit and function.
- Create space at a team meeting to reflect: *Where did we see fruit this week? How did it show up in customer experience?*

Prayer

Lord, teach me to value what You value. In a world obsessed with numbers, help me stay anchored in fruit. Show me how to measure with grace, to evaluate with eternity in mind, and to lead others with Your wisdom.   May our metrics reflect Heaven's priorities, not just results, but relationships. Not just speed, but Spirit. In all we do, may You be glorified. Amen.

Chapter 18
Language That Builds the House

Spiritual Principle: *Words create worlds, speak with wisdom, build with grace*

Scripture Anchor: 'Death and life are in the power of the tongue, and those who love it will eat its fruit.' – Proverbs 18:21 (ESV)

The way we speak, especially *behind the scenes*, shapes what people believe is acceptable, true, and good. Language doesn't just describe culture. It creates it.

Every organization is built by words:

- The ones we say in staff meetings.
- The ones we whisper in hallways.
- The ones we send in Zoom, emails, and group chats.
- The ones we *don't* say when truth is needed most.

In customer experience teams, communication is often fast, reactive, and emotionally charged. There's pressure, there's mess, and there's the temptation to vent instead of build. But Scripture reminds us that every word is a   seed, and what we plant, we eventually harvest.

Death and life are in the power of the tongue.

That means our internal culture will reflect our internal conversations.   If our communication is:

- Cynical, our culture will grow bitter.
- Gossip-filled, our culture will grow divided.
- Hope-filled, our culture will grow resilient.
- Honest and gracious, our culture will grow healthy.

This doesn't mean we avoid hard truths. It means we deliver them with love. It means we ask questions before making assumptions. It means we model communication that reflects the humility, clarity, and truth of Jesus.

Jesus never used language to shame. Even when rebuking, He called people up, not out. He corrected the Pharisees publicly because of their pride, and He corrected His disciples privately because of their hearts. His   words were always perfectly suited to the person and the purpose.

The words you speak as a leader or team member are not neutral. They are either laying bricks or creating cracks. *Are your words building the house? Or breaking it down?*

Study Guide: Language That Builds the House Key Scriptures to Meditate On

- Proverbs 18:21 – *"Death and life are in the power of the tongue."*

- Ephesians 4:29 – *"Let no unwholesome word proceed from your mouth…"*
- James 3:9–10 – *"With the tongue we bless our Lord… and curse people…"*

Reflection Questions

1. What is the tone of my communication with my team? With peers? Behind closed doors?
2. Do I speak differently about people when they're not present? What does that reveal?
3. How often do I use words to build someone up, even when correction is needed?
4. What kinds of communication habits have been modeled by leadership? What have I passed on?
5. What would change if I saw every internal conversation as part of my ministry?

Practical Application

- Conduct a "communication audit" this week. Review a few internal messages (emails, chats, meetings)   and ask: *Did this build unity? Did it reflect truth and grace?*
- Set a new tone by beginning one team communication this week with a word of blessing or encouragement.

Prayer

Lord, teach me to speak like You. Let my words be vessels of truth, healing, and grace. Show me where I've used language to divide or diminish, and help me make it right. Use my communication to shape a culture that   reflects Heaven. Help me speak life into systems, teams, and hearts. Let my words build the house You are   building. Amen.

Chapter 19
Making Peace, Keeping Unity

Spiritual Principle: *Peace isn't the absence of conflict, it's the presence of righteousness*

Scripture Anchor: "Blessed are the peacemakers, for they shall be called children of God." – Matthew 5:9 (NIV)

Conflict is not the enemy.

Unresolved conflict is.

In any environment, especially in customer experience where emotions often run high, conflict will arise. Between customers and agents. Between teammates. Between departments. Even between leadership and   frontline workers.

But the goal in a Kingdom culture is not avoiding conflict at all costs.

It's handling conflict with courage, humility, and love, so that unity grows stronger, not weaker.

Jesus calls us to be peacemakers, not peacekeepers. Peacekeepers avoid confrontation to maintain surface-level calm.

Peacemakers step into confrontation to pursue real reconciliation.   Biblical conflict resolution means:

- Facing the issue directly but gently.
- Prioritizing restoration over being "right."
- Listening before defending.
- Speaking truth without rage, love without compromise.

In Matthew 18, Jesus lays out a clear and practical roadmap for resolving conflict:

1. Go directly to the person in private.
2. If unresolved, bring one or two others as witnesses.
3. If still unresolved, involve wider accountability (leadership, church authority).

This process models respect, patience, and escalation only when needed, not gossip, slander, or passive aggression. In customer experience, biblical conflict resolution applies to:

- Handling customer escalations with listening, validation, and boundaries.
- Addressing internal team issues early, before bitterness takes root.
- Leading team conversations about mistakes with truth *and* grace.
- Creating a culture where people feel safe to disagree, and safe to reconcile.

I remember a situation where a team member misunderstood a policy change and felt betrayed. Instead of letting it fester, we sat down face to face. We listened. We clarified. We apologized where we needed to. We prayed together. What could have created permanent division instead built deeper loyalty.

Conflict, handled God's way, produces fruit.

Unity is not about perfect agreement. It's about shared commitment to love, truth, and mission, even when it's messy.

Study Guide: Making Peace, Keeping Unity Key Scriptures to Meditate On

- Matthew 5:9 – *"Blessed are the peacemakers…"*
- Matthew 18:15–17 – *Jesus' steps for resolving conflict.*
- Romans 12:18 – *"As far as it depends on you, live at peace with everyone."*

Reflection Questions

1. How do I typically respond to conflict: by avoiding it, attacking, or addressing it biblically?
2. Is there unresolved conflict in my workplace or team that God is calling me to address?
3. How can I approach difficult conversations with both truth and grace?
4. What systems or practices could help normalize healthy conflict resolution in my organization?
5. How can I model peacemaking, not just peacekeeping, in daily leadership?

Practical Application

- Identify one unresolved conflict or tension point. Pray about it. Then take one step toward biblical reconciliation this week, whether it's scheduling a conversation, offering forgiveness, or clearing a misunderstanding.
- Introduce Matthew 18 principles into your team's communication norms: Direct. Private. Gentle. Redemptive.

Prayer

Father, You are the God of reconciliation. You made peace with me through Christ, and You call me to make peace with others. Teach me to be a peacemaker, not by avoiding conflict, but by facing it with Your heart. Give me humility to listen, wisdom to speak, and courage to restore. Let unity in my words, my team, and my work reflect the unity of Your Spirit. Amen.

Chapter 20
Building a Legacy of Service

Spiritual Principle: *Kingdom work is never wasted, it echoes into eternity*
Scripture Anchor: 'Only one life, 'twill soon be past; only what's done for Christ will last.' (Inspired by Matthew 6:19–21: "Lay up for yourselves treasures in heaven…")

It's easy to fall into the trap of serving for today's applause. The five-star review.

The quarterly bonus.

The customer satisfaction score.

But Kingdom service isn't measured in likes, metrics, or trophies. It's measured in legacy.

When you serve with the heart of Christ, even the smallest acts, an encouraging word, a prayer whispered for a customer, a decision made with integrity when no one is watching, are building something eternal.

Jesus constantly modeled generational vision. When He healed, He also taught. When He served, He also commissioned. He wasn't just building a movement for that moment, He was establishing a Kingdom for generations to come.

In customer experience, it's easy to think in terms of transactions. But every transaction is an opportunity for transformation.

You may think you're just resolving an issue, but you're sowing trust.

You may think you're just handling a return, but you're showing what forgiveness looks like. You may think you're just offering a policy, but you're offering a glimpse of mercy.

Legacy-building service means:

- Seeing beyond the moment into the soul.
- Choosing faithfulness even when results are slow.
- Investing in people, not just processes.
- Leading with eternity in mind, not just efficiency.

I remember speaking with a seasoned customer experience agent who said, *'I just treat every call like it could change someone's day, or their life.'* He never became "famous." He wasn't trying to climb a ladder. But his impact was deep, rippling through thousands of interactions with patience, kindness, and hope.

He built a legacy.

Legacy is built one unseen, faithful, Spirit-led step at a time. You don't have to see the fruit today.

You just have to sow the seed today.

And trust the God who brings the harvest.

Study Guide: Building a Legacy of Service Key Scriptures to Meditate On

- Matthew 6:19–21 – *"Lay up treasures in heaven…"*

- Galatians 6:9 – *"Let us not grow weary in doing good…"*
- 1 Corinthians 3:6–8 – *"One plants, another waters, but God gives the growth."*

Reflection Questions

1. Am I focused more on short-term results or long-term, eternal impact in my service and leadership?
2. What kind of legacy am I building through the way I treat people daily?
3. How does seeing service as eternal investment change the way I approach "small" tasks?
4. Who modeled legacy-minded service for me? What did their life teach me?
5. What seeds can I intentionally plant today, even if I never see the harvest?

Practical Application

- Write a personal "Service Legacy Statement" – a few sentences that describe the impact you want your work and life to leave behind. Keep it visible as a reminder.
- Celebrate someone this week who serves faithfully behind the scenes, publicly honor their "hidden" work as a model of Kingdom legacy.

Prayer

Father, thank You that nothing done in love is ever wasted. Teach me to build with eternity in mind. Help me to see every task, every word, every interaction as a seed You can use for a harvest I may never see. Strengthen me to stay faithful, even when results are slow. May my service today echo into generations tomorrow, and may it all point back to You. Amen.

Part 3
**Integration – Culture, Systems & People, Where Everything
We've Built Internally (Heart Posture) And Externally
(Practical Service) Gets Fully *Woven into the
Organizational DNA*.**

Chapter 21
Weaving Faith into the Fabric

Spiritual Principle: *Faith isn't just spoken, it's sewn into every detail*

> **Scripture Anchor: 'And whatever you do, whether in word or deed, do it all in the name of the Lord Jesus.'**
> − *Colossians 3:17 (NIV)*

It's one thing to personally embody the fruit of the Spirit in your work.

It's another thing to weave that Spirit into the very structure, culture, and systems of your organization.

True Kingdom culture doesn't rely on a few passionate people.

It's woven into the policies, the meetings, the trainings, the celebrations, the correction, and even the "small print."

It's sewn into the tone of the onboarding packet.

It's embedded in how managers coach, how teams debrief, and how conflicts are handled.

It's the thread running through every customer policy, every staff memo, and every internal report. It's faith that's not compartmentalized to private belief but integrated into public action.

Paul's command in Colossians 3:17 is simple and revolutionary: Whatever you do, in word or deed, do it all in the name of Jesus.

Not some. Not most. All.

What does weaving faith into the fabric look like in practice?

- **Hiring for heart:** Prioritizing humility, teachability, and spirit over just technical skills.
- **Training for transformation:** Embedding values and character into every new employee's journey.
- **Leading with prayer:** Making prayer a natural, consistent rhythm in leadership meetings and big decisions.
- **Correcting with compassion:** Upholding truth without abandoning mercy.
- **Celebrating fruit:** Honoring patience, faithfulness, and kindness, not just sales numbers.
- **Structuring for service:** Designing workflows and systems that prioritize people over efficiency alone.
- **Communicating with consistency:** Reinforcing mission and vision in every announcement and update.
- **Restoring when wronged:** Modeling forgiveness corporately when mistakes are made internally or externally.

When you weave faith into the systems themselves, you no longer rely on individual personalities to carry the culture. The culture carries itself, because it's built into the foundation.

It's no longer just good customer service. It's Gospel-shaped service.

It's no longer just good leadership. It's Kingdom leadership.

And it's no longer just doing business.

It's doing ministry through business, even if your product is packages, policies, or spreadsheets.

This is how the radical thread of faith becomes unbreakable in the fabric of your customer experience and leadership model.

It's how ordinary systems become extraordinary testimonies. It's how daily work becomes sacred worship.

Study Guide: Weaving Faith into the Fabric Key Scriptures to Meditate On

- Colossians 3:17 – *"Do it all in the name of the Lord Jesus…"*
- Matthew 5:16 – *"Let your light shine before others…"*
- 1 Corinthians 10:31 – *"Whether you eat or drink… do it all for the glory of God."*

Reflection Questions

1. Which parts of our organizational systems currently reflect Kingdom values well?
2. Which areas feel disconnected from faith, and how might they be re-aligned?
3. How can prayer, encouragement, and discipleship be woven more deeply into our team rhythms?
4. If an outsider experienced our company culture, what story would they hear without us saying a word?
5. What's one small but powerful place I can sew faith into the fabric this week?

Practical Application

- Identify one system (onboarding, customer service process, employee communication, etc.) and   prayerfully review it: *Does this reflect our faith or just our function?* Make one adjustment to better   reflect Kingdom values.
- Start a small initiative, like monthly prayer gatherings, servant leadership training, or Kingdom KPI   tracking, to help weave faith visibly and practically into your team's rhythms.

Prayer

Jesus, You are not a part of my life, you are the whole foundation. Help me to weave You into everything: every word, every system, every plan. Let no part of our work be secular and separate. Teach me to build culture and systems that carry Your heart. Let the fabric of our organization be a tapestry of Your grace, truth, and love.

May people encounter You through what we create. Amen.

Chapter 22
On Earth as It Is in Heaven

Spiritual Principle: *Customer experience can be a glimpse of the Kingdom*

Scripture Anchor: 'Your kingdom come, Your will be done, on earth as it is in heaven.' – Matthew 6:10 (NIV)

When Jesus taught His disciples to pray, He taught them to ask not just for strength or provision, but for Heaven to touch Earth.

"Your kingdom come. Your will be done. On earth as it is in heaven."

Heaven is not just a future hope, it's a present invitation.

And if that's true, then customer experience, the everyday, ordinary interactions people have with your organization, can actually become a portal where the culture of Heaven touches the earth.

What is Heaven like?

- Full of peace, not anxiety.
- Full of abundance, not scarcity.
- Full of dignity, not dismissal.
- Full of joy, not drudgery.
- Full of restoration, not rejection.

Imagine if every customer, every vendor, every partner walked away from an interaction with your company feeling even a fraction of that.

That's what it means to build customer experience "on earth as it is in heaven."

Heavenly customer experience isn't just about pleasing customers. It's about honoring their value as image-bearers of God.

It's about designing systems and interactions that:

- Choose restoration over rigid rules when possible.
- Reflect joy even in tough conversations.
- Treat mistakes with grace without compromising truth.
- Prioritize personal connection over robotic efficiency.
- Slow blessings instead of burnout.

One powerful example comes from the early Church. In Acts 2, believers shared all things in common, meeting needs so radically that "they enjoyed the favor of all the people." Their way of living *was itself* the witness.

Our way of serving can be the same.

When a customer calls in worried and stressed, they should encounter someone who carries *peace*. When an order goes wrong, and disappointment could turn into anger, the response should offer *gentleness* and *solution*. When confusion or miscommunication arises, the culture should offer *clarity* without *condescension*.

And when gratitude flows back from a customer or client, it should be received not with pride, but with praise to the Father, because the light shining wasn't ours to begin with.

We are not just answering emails or shipping products.

We are building a culture that makes people feel a little closer to the heart of God.

Study Guide: On Earth as It Is in Heaven Key Scriptures to Meditate On

- Matthew 6:10 – *"Your kingdom come, Your will be done, on earth as it is in heaven."*
- Acts 2:42–47 – *The favor and growth of the early Church.*
- 2 Corinthians 5:20 – *"We are therefore Christ's ambassadors…"*

Reflection Questions

- What emotions and experiences do people consistently have when they interact with my organization?
- How closely do those experiences mirror the peace, joy, dignity, and abundance of Heaven?
- Where in our service could we offer a taste of Heaven, especially in difficult situations?
- How can I personally embody the culture of Heaven when interacting with customers or coworkers?
- What systems, policies, or habits might need to change to reflect a Kingdom experience more fully?

Practical Application

- Walk through your customer journey from start to finish as if you were a guest in the Kingdom of Heaven. Where does it need more peace? More patience? More generosity?
- Create a "Kingdom Experience" checklist for your team: small but meaningful ways to reflect Heaven in every customer interaction (e.g., start every interaction with warmth, end every interaction with a blessing).

Prayer

Father, Your Kingdom is full of goodness, truth, joy, and love. Teach me to build spaces, systems, and experiences that reflect Your heart. Let our customer interactions be places where peace is felt, dignity is restored, and joy is contagious. Help me to see service not as a chore, but as an extension of Heaven's welcome. Use my hands, my voice, and my heart to make Your Kingdom visible, one interaction at a time. Amen.

Chapter 23
People Over Performance

Spiritual Principle: *Growth means nothing if love gets lost*

Scripture Anchor: 'If I have…all knowledge, and if I have a faith that can move mountains, but do not have love, I am nothing.' – 1 Corinthians 13:2 (NIV)

Performance matters. Results matter.

Excellence matters.

But people matter more.

Without love, the greatest achievements amount to nothing.

As organizations grow, it's easy, so easy, for the metrics to start taking precedence over the men and women carrying them.

- We celebrate speed over sincerity.
- We reward numbers over nurture.
- We pursue results at the expense of relationship.

And when that happens, the culture subtly shifts from a Kingdom culture to a corporate one. From shepherding to managing.

From building people to using people. This is not the way of Jesus.

Jesus grew movements that changed history, but He never treated people as means to an end. He noticed the invisible ones in the crowd.

He paused for the woman at the well even though an entire city waited for Him. He restored Peter personally before releasing him publicly.

He never sacrificed the soul for the sake of speed.

In customer experience and leadership today, honoring people over performance looks like:

- Protecting human dignity in moments of failure.
- Valuing rest and health as much as productivity.
- Celebrating unseen faithfulness, not just visible wins.
- Refusing to exploit exhaustion in the name of "hustle."
- Creating accountability systems that build, not break.
- There will be seasons where numbers matter. When efficiency must improve. When tough calls must be made. But those moments must always bow to the higher call of love.

When love leads, excellence follows, but it is excellence rooted in wholeness, not fear. When love leads, correction restores instead of crushing.

When love leads, customer experience stops being about transactions, and starts being about transformation. We are called to lead like shepherds, not just drive outcomes.

Because in the Kingdom, the question isn't simply, *"What did we accomplish?"*
It's also, *"Who did we become along the way?"*

Study Guide: People Over Performance Key Scriptures to Meditate On

- 1 Corinthians 13:2 – *"If I have… all knowledge… but do not have love, I am nothing."*
- John 10:11 – *"I am the good shepherd. The good shepherd lays down His life for the sheep."*
- 1 Thessalonians 2:8 – *"We loved you so much that we were delighted to share with you not only the gospel of God but our lives as well."*

Reflection Questions

1. In our current culture, where are we at risk of valuing performance over people?
2. How do our incentives, promotions, or celebrations reflect (or fail to reflect) our values?
3. What would it look like to honor the human side of business, even in seasons of high growth?
4. How can I personally affirm someone's worth beyond their productivity this week?
5. Am I willing to choose a slower path to success if it means keeping love at the center?

Practical Application

- Send an unexpected note of encouragement or gratitude to a team member, not for a measurable success, but simply for their faithfulness, kindness, or growth.
- In your next leadership or service meeting, celebrate a story where love was prioritized over "winning", even if the world would consider it less impressive.

———————— ✦ ————————

Prayer

Father, keep my heart anchored in Your love. Teach me to value people the way You do, to see their worth apart from their work. Help me to lead, build, and serve in ways that honor Your heart, not just my goals. Let my leadership create spaces where people flourish, not just produce. Let everything I build be shaped by love.
Amen.

———————— ✦ ————————

Chapter 24
Training for Transformation

Spiritual Principle: *True leadership development is discipleship*

Scripture Anchor: 'Go therefore and make disciples of all nations, teaching them to observe all that I have commanded you.' – Matthew 28:19–20 (ESV)

In most organizations, training means equipping someone with the right knowledge, skills, and procedures to succeed in their role.

In the Kingdom, training goes deeper. It's discipleship.

Jesus never merely trained His followers to perform tasks.

He transformed them, through teaching, correction, example, prayer, and relationship, until their inner character matched their outer calling.

If we want a culture that truly reflects Christ, we cannot settle for surface-level development:

- Checklists without convictions.
- Techniques without transformation.
- Policies without purpose.

Transformation comes when people are not just told what to do, but shown how to become. That's why training in a Kingdom-centered customer experience culture must focus on both:

- Skill development (the excellence of work) and
- Heart development (the excellence of spirit).

This kind of training is slower. It's messier. It requires investment, patience, and relational trust. But it produces servants, not just workers. Leaders, not just managers. Disciples, not just employees.

Training for transformation looks like:

- Modeling humility and repentance when leaders make mistakes.
- Offering feedback that calls out potential, not just problems.
- Mentoring new team members through prayer, encouragement, and truth.
- Reinforcing identity in Christ, not just role performance.

One of the best leadership development practices I ever witnessed wasn't a workshop or seminar, it was a quiet leader who would end every coaching session by asking, *"How's your heart?"*

Not just, *"How's your quota?"* How's your heart?

Because if we don't shape hearts, it's only a matter of time before skills collapse under the weight of unhealed brokenness.

Jesus commissioned His disciples to teach others to observe all He commanded, not just head knowledge, but life alignment.

Training for transformation follows that same pattern:

- Teach truth.
- Model truth.
- Walk alongside.
- Call people higher.

And when we do, we don't just create better workers.

We create Kingdom carriers, people who will lead others to the heart of God through their work, their service, and their lives.

Study Guide: Training for Transformation Key Scriptures to Meditate On

1. Matthew 28:19–20 – *"Make disciples of all nations…"*
2. 2 Timothy 2:2 – *"Entrust to faithful people who will teach others also."*
3. Colossians 1:28 – *"We proclaim Him, admonishing and teaching everyone with all wisdom…"*

Reflection Questions

1. Do I train people simply for tasks, or am I helping shape their character?
2. How often do our training programs address the heart, not just the hands?
3. Who in my sphere needs not just information, but encouragement and spiritual investment?
4. Am I willing to prioritize transformation even when it requires more time, effort, and patience?
5. What practices could we add to our training to reinforce spiritual growth, not just job skills?

Practical Application

- Integrate a simple "heart" check-in into your training programs (e.g., questions about encouragement, gratitude, service mindset).
- Identify one person you're training or mentoring. Invest intentionally in *their heart*, not just their skill, through encouragement, prayer, truth, and walking with them.

Prayer

Lord Jesus, You are the Master Teacher. You shape hearts before You shape hands. Teach me to train and develop others the way You do, with patience, love, and eternal vision. Help me to see the gold inside people and call it forth. Let every training session, every coaching moment, and every act of leadership be a doorway for Your Spirit to work. Transform us from the inside out, and let us reflect Your heart in all we do.

Amen.

Chapter 25
The Thread That Holds It All Together

Spiritual Principle: *Christ is not part of the fabric, He is the fabric*

Scripture Anchor: 'He is before all things, and in Him all things hold together.' – Colossians 1:17 (NIV)

Every system. Every policy. Every interaction.

Every moment of service.

It all either falls apart, or holds together, based on one thing: Who is at the center.

Without Christ, customer experience becomes survival. Without Christ, leadership becomes control.

Without Christ, service becomes performance.

But with Christ? Service becomes sacred.

Leadership becomes stewardship.

Customer experience becomes Kingdom-building.

Throughout this journey, we have talked about heart posture, practical systems, relational culture, leadership discipline, communication, conflict, growth, and legacy. We have threaded biblical principles through every   layer of customer and employee experience.

But hear this clearly: Jesus is not one thread among many. He is the thread.

He is the one who weaves wholeness into broken teams. He is the one who binds love into leadership.

He is the one who ties grace into policy.

He is the one who knits joy into daily service. He is the one who mends mistakes with mercy.

He is the one who sews courage into weary hearts.

He is the one who fastens together a culture that no storm can tear apart.

Without Christ holding the fabric together, everything will fray in time. Ego will creep in.

Bitterness will build. Systems will crumble.

But when Christ is exalted, not just in our mission statements, but in our real, everyday actions, He breathes life into the work of our hands.

This is not easy work. You will face resistance.

You will have days where love feels costly, and where faithfulness feels unnoticed.

But this work matters. This weaving matters.

Because it tells the world something about the One who sent you.

Every email answered with patience. Every policy written with compassion.

Every hard conversation navigated with truth and grace. Every correction offered with dignity.

Every unseen act of service.

All of it stitches together a testimony: Jesus is real. His Kingdom is real. His love changes everything.

And when we weave Him into every thread of our work, our leadership, our culture, He doesn't just hold it together.

He makes it beautiful.

Study Guide: The Thread That Holds It All Together Key Scriptures to Meditate On

- Colossians 1:17 – *"He is before all things, and in Him all things hold together."*
- John 15:5 – *"Apart from Me you can do nothing."*
- Revelation 21:5 – *"Behold, I am making all things new."*

Reflection Questions

- Is Christ truly at the center of my work, or have I placed something else there?
- What parts of my service or leadership need to be re-centered around Him?
- How has Jesus held me, and my work, together when I felt like falling apart?
- How can I help weave His presence deeper into the fabric of my team or organization?
- What testimony do I want the tapestry of my service to tell when the story is complete?

Practical Application

- Prayerfully re-dedicate your work, every task, conversation, and decision, to Christ this week. Invite Him to weave Himself even deeper into every layer.
- Create a visible reminder (a verse, a phrase, a symbol) somewhere in your workspace to keep your focus centered on Him daily.

———————— ✦ ————————

Prayer

Jesus, You are the thread that holds everything together. Forgive me when I try to stitch things together in my own strength. Teach me to weave You into every fiber of my work, my leadership, my service. Let every part of my life be a testimony of Your goodness, Your love, and Your faithfulness. Hold it all together. Make it beautiful in Your hands. I surrender it all to You.

Amen.

———————— ✦ ————————

A Letter to You, Fellow Weaver of Faith

Dear Friend,

If you are reading this, it means you stayed with me until the final thread was woven.

And I want to take a moment, not as an author speaking to a reader, but as a fellow servant, to say: Thank you.

Thank you for daring to believe that business can be sacred.

Thank you for being willing to examine not just what you do, but who you are becoming.

Thank you for daring to weave faith, love, and service into places where the world expects performance, pressure, and profit.

You are part of a radical movement.

A movement that says customers are not just accounts, they are beloved souls.

A movement that says employees are not just resources, they are image-bearers of a living God.

A movement that says service is not just what we do, it's who we are, because Christ served us first.

There will be days ahead where this calling will feel heavy. Days when shortcuts seem easier.

Days when love costs more than applause.

Days when you wonder if the small kindnesses, the unseen faithfulness, the prayer-whispered decisions are making any real difference.

Please hear me: they are.

In the Kingdom of God, nothing done in love is ever wasted.

Every seed you plant, every stitch you weave, every weary prayer you lift matters more than you can see.

You are building more than a company. You are building a legacy.

You are threading Heaven into Earth, one faithful decision at a time.

And someday, maybe when you're still here, maybe when you stand before Jesus, you will see the tapestry that was woven through your hands.

You will see the faces of those who felt His love through your service.

You will hear the stories of those who were touched by a kindness you barely remember offering. You will realize: it was never just about service. It was always about salvation.

It was always about Him.

So keep weaving, my friend. Even when the thread feels thin.

Even when the loom creaks under the weight. Even when the pattern isn't fully clear.

Keep weaving.

Because you are part of something bigger than yourself.

You are part of the radical thread of faith, love, and service that the world so desperately needs. And you are not weaving alone.

I'm standing with you.

The angels are cheering you on.

And the One who called you is faithful. He is the Master Weaver.

And He will complete what He started.

With love, hope, and unwavering faith, Karen

Final Commissioning Prayer

Father,

Thank You for the one who holds this book, whose heart burns with a desire to serve You faithfully through their work.

I pray that You would anoint their hands to weave well. Anoint their voice to speak life.

Anoint their heart to lead with love.

When discouragement whispers, drown it out with Your promises. When exhaustion creeps in, refresh them with Your Spirit.

When fear rises up, anchor them in Your courage.

May every customer, every coworker, every unseen observer encounter a glimpse of You through them. May their service shake foundations.

May their faithfulness ripple through generations.

May their leadership open doors for Your Kingdom to come, on earth as it is in Heaven.

Weave them into Your grand tapestry, Lord. Use them for Your glory.

And when the weaving is done, may they hear the only words that matter:

"Well done, good and faithful servant."

In Jesus' name, Amen.

Resource and Study Guide

For Personal Growth, Team Studies, and Leadership Workshops

Congratulations on completing *The Radical Thread*!

But the journey of weaving faith, love, and service into customer experience has only just begun.

This Resource and Study Guide is designed to help you

- Reflect deeply on the principles you've learned.
- Apply these truths practically in your daily work.
- Equip your teams and organizations to build cultures that reflect Heaven.
- Grow into a leader who leads hearts, not just processes.

You can use it

- For personal devotion and reflection.
- As a leadership book club study.
- In team training sessions.
- As the foundation for service leadership workshops.

Personal Reflection Journey Instructions

After reading each chapter, pause and reflect using the following questions. Journal your answers, pray through them, and revisit them as you grow.

Core Reflection Questions for Every Chapter

- What new insight did God reveal to me through this chapter?
- How can I apply this principle practically in my work this week?
- Where am I tempted to lead out of fear, pride, or performance instead of love and service?
- Who can I bless, encourage, or disciple using this principle?
- What step of obedience is the Holy Spirit asking me to take based on what I just learned?

Challenge

Pick one practical action from each chapter's study guide and complete it within the week. Watch how small   acts of obedience build a radical culture over time.

Group Study Questions

Instructions

Use these questions in small groups, leadership circles, team book clubs, or discipleship gatherings to deepen discussion and application.

- What chapter resonated most deeply with you, and why?
- How would our customer experience change if we truly built it around [Chapter Topic , e.g., abundance, joy, forgiveness]?

- What barriers do we face when trying to live out this principle practically?
- How can we encourage one another when it becomes hard to weave faith into ordinary tasks?
- What system, policy, or process could we revise to better reflect the Spirit of Christ?
- How can we hold each other accountable to building Kingdom culture, not just great performance?
- Where have you seen glimpses of "Heaven touching Earth" in your work?
- How can we pray for each other as we continue to weave the radical thread in our daily lives?

Leadership Workshop Ideas

Host a Service Leadership Day or Customer Experience Retreat!

Ideas to bring the book principles to life for your team:

Workshop Element	Description
Devotional Kickoff	**Begin with Colossians 3:17 or John 15 and prayer**
Storytelling Session	**Team shares experiences of service that impacted lives**
Role-Play Scenarios	**Practice customer interactions with truth + love.**
"Acts of Service" Exercise	**Leaders practice humility and support by engaging in meaningful actions that place the needs of their team first**
Policy Review Workshop	**Redesign a few customer policies through a Kingdom lens**
Legacy Mapping	**Each person writes down the legacy they want to leave through service**
Worship and Commissioning	**End with worship, prayer, and blessing over the team**

Scripture Meditation Plan

A 25-Day Radical Thread Scripture Journey

(1 passage per day , match each chapter)

Day	Scripture Focus	Theme
1	**John 10:10**	**Abundance**
2	**Colossians 3:23**	**Service as worship**
3	**Romans 12:15**	**Presence**
4	**Proverbs 15:1**	**Gentleness**
5	**2 Corinthians 12:9**	**Grace in tension**
6	**Ephesians 4:15**	**Truth in love**
7	**Galatians 6:9**	**Endurance**
8	**Nehemiah 8:10**	**Joy as strength**
9	**Ephesians 4:32**	**Forgiveness**
10	**Galatians 5:22–23**	**Spiritual fruit**

11	Matthew 24:45–46	Steward leadership
12	1 Corinthians 12:27	Belonging
13	Matthew 20:26	Servant leadership
14	Philippians 4:9	Training for transformation
15	Micah 6:8	Building just, merciful system
16	Revelation 3:19	Correction that restores
17	Matthew 7:16	Measuring by fruit
18	Proverbs 18:21	Life-giving communication
19	Matthew 5:9	Peacemaking
20	Matthew 6:19–21	Building a legacy
21	Colossians 3:17	Weaving faith into systems
22	Matthew 6:10	Heaven touching Earth
23	1 Corinthians 13:2	People over performance
24	Matthew 28:19–20	Discipling, not just developing
25	Colossians 1:17	Christ holds it all together

References

(Primary Biblical References Cited Throughout the Book)

- John 10:10 – Life abundantly
- Colossians 3:23 – Work heartily for the Lord
- Romans 12:15 – Rejoice with those who rejoice
- Proverbs 15:1 – A gentle answer turns away wrath
- 2 Corinthians 12:9 – Grace is sufficient
- Ephesians 4:15 – Speaking the truth in love
- Galatians 6:9 – Do not grow weary of doing good
- Nehemiah 8:10 – The joy of the Lord is your strength
- Ephesians 4:32 – Forgiving one another
- Galatians 5:22–23 – Fruit of the Spirit
- Matthew 24:45–46 – Faithful stewardship
- 1 Corinthians 12:27 – The body of Christ
- Matthew 20:26 – Servant leadership
- Philippians 4:9 – Practice what you have seen and heard
- Micah 6:8 – Act justly, love mercy, walk humbly
- Revelation 3:19 – Those God loves, He disciplines
- Matthew 7:16 – Recognize them by their fruit
- Proverbs 18:21 – Power of the tongue
- Matthew 5:9 – Blessed are the peacemakers
- Matthew 6:19–21 – Treasures in Heaven
- Matthew 6:10 – Your Kingdom come, Your will be done
- 1 Corinthians 13:2 – Without love, I am nothing
- Matthew 28:19–20 – Make disciples of all nations
- Colossians 1:17 – Christ holds all things together

(All Scripture quotations are taken from the English Standard Version (ESV) or New International Version (NIV) unless otherwise noted.)

Back Cover Description The Radical Thread

Weaving Faith, Love, and Service into the Customer Experience

What if every interaction, every email, every meeting, every customer conversation, could become an opportunity to weave Heaven into Earth?

In *The Radical Thread*, you'll discover a revolutionary approach to customer experience rooted not in performance, but in faith, love, and Spirit-led service.

More than a business strategy, *The Radical Thread* is a call to discipleship through daily work, a reminder that every task can carry eternal weight when it's done in the name of Jesus.

It's time to stop compartmentalizing your faith and start weaving it into every thread. You were made to lead a different way. The world is ready.